Isaac Newton

Four Letters From Sir Isaac Newton to Doctor Bentley

Containing Some Arguments in Proof of a Deity

Isaac Newton

Four Letters From Sir Isaac Newton to Doctor Bentley
Containing Some Arguments in Proof of a Deity

ISBN/EAN: 9783744657372

Printed in Europe, USA, Canada, Australia, Japan

Cover: Foto ©Lupo / pixelio.de

More available books at **www.hansebooks.com**

FOUR
LETTERS
FROM
SIR ISAAC NEWTON
TO
DOCTOR BENTLEY.

CONTAINING

SOME **ARGUMENTS**

IN

PROOF of a **DEITY**.

LONDON:

Printed for R. and J. DODSLEY, *Pall-Mall,*

M DCC LVI.

LETTERS, &c.

LETTER I.

To the Reverend Dr. RICHARD BENTLEY, *at the Bishop of* Worcester's *House in* Park-street, Westminster.

SIR,

WHEN I wrote my Treatise about our System, I had an Eye upon such Principles as might work with considering Men, for the Belief of a Deity, and nothing can rejoice me more than to find it useful for that Purpose. But if I

B   have

have done the Public any Service this way, it is due to nothing but Induſtry and patient Thought.

As to your firſt Query, it ſeems to me that if the Matter of our Sun and Planets, and all the Matter of the Univerſe, were evenly ſcattered throughout all the Heavens, and every Particle had an innate Gravity towards all the reſt, and the whole Space, throughout which this Matter was ſcattered, was but finite, the Matter on the outſide of this Space would by its Gravity tend towards all the Matter on the inſide, and by conſequence fall down into the middle of the whole Space, and there compoſe one great ſpherical Maſs. But if the Matter was evenly diſpoſed throughout an infinite Space, it could never convene into one Maſs, but ſome of it would convene into one Maſs and ſome into another, ſo as to make an infinite Number of great Maſſes, ſcattered at great Diſtances from one to another through-

throughout all that infinite Space. And thus might the Sun and fixt Stars be formed, suppofing the Matter were of a lucid Nature. But how the Matter fhould divide itfelf into two forts, and that Part of it, which is fit to compofe a fhining Body, fhould fall down into one Mafs and make a Sun, and the reft, which is fit to compofe an opaque Body, fhould coalefce, not into one great Body, like the fhining Matter, but into many little ones; or if the Sun at firft were an opaque Body like the Planets, or the Planets lucid Bodies like the Sun, how he alone fhould be changed into a fhining Body, whilft all they continue opaque, or all they be changed into opaque ones, whilft he remains unchanged, I do not think explicable by meer natural Caufes, but am forced to afcribe it to the Counfel and Contrivance of a voluntary Agent.

The fame Power, whether natural or fupernatural, which placed the Sun in

the

the Center of the fix primary Planets, placed *Saturn* in the Center of the Orbs of his five fecondary Planets, and *Jupiter* in the Center of his four fecondary Planets, and the Earth in the Center of the Moon's Orb; and therefore had this Caufe been a blind one, without Contrivance or Defign, the Sun would have been a Body of the fame kind with *Saturn*, *Jupiter*, and the Earth, that is, without Light and Heat. Why there is one Body in our Syftem qualified to give Light and Heat to all the reft, I know no Reafon, but becaufe the Author of the Syftem thought it convenient, and why there is but one Body of this kind I know no Reafon, but becaufe one was fufficient to warm and enlighten all the reft. For the *Cartefian* Hypothefis of Suns lofing their Light, and then turning into Comets, and Comets into Planets, can have no Place in my Syftem, and is plainly erroneous; becaufe it is certain that as often as they appear to us, they defcend into the Syftem

of

of our Planets, lower than the Orb of
Jupiter, and fometimes lower than the
Orbs of *Venus* and *Mercury*, and yet never
ftay here, but always return from the Sun
with the fame Degrees of Motion by
which they approached him.

To your fecond Query, I anfwer, that
the Motions which the Planets now have
could not fpring from any natural Caufe
alone, but were impreffed by an intelligent Agent. For fince Comets defcend
into the Region of our Planets, and here
move all manner of ways, going fometimes the fame way with the Planets,
fometimes the contrary way, and fometimes in crofs ways, in Planes inclined to
the Plane of the Ecliptick, and at all
kinds of Angles, 'tis plain that there is
no natural Caufe which could determine
all the Planets, both primary and fecondary, to move the fame way and in
the fame Plane, without any confiderable
Variation : This muft have been the Effect

fect of Counfel. Nor is there any natural
Caufe which could give the Planets thofe
juft Degrees of Velocity, in Proportion
to their Diftances from the Sun, and other
central Bodies, which were requifite to
make them move in fuch concentrick
Orbs about thofe Bodies. Had the Planets
been as fwift as Comets, in Proportion to
their Diftances from the Sun (as they
would have been, had their Motion been
caufed by their Gravity, whereby the
Matter, at the firft Formation of the
Planets, might fall from the remoteft Re-
gions towards the Sun) they would not
move in concentrick Orbs, but in fuch
eccentrick ones as the Comets move in.
Were all the Planets as fwift as *Mercury*,
or as flow as *Saturn* or his Satellites; or
were their feveral Velocities otherwife
much greater or lefs than they are, as
they might have been had they arofe from
any other Caufe than their Gravities; or
had the Diftances from the Centers a-
bout which they move, been greater or
lefs

lefs than they are with the fame Velocities; or had the Quantity of Matter in
the Sun, or in *Saturn*, *Jupiter*, and the
Earth, and by confequence their gravitating Power been greater or lefs than it is,
the primary Planets could not have re-
volved about the Sun, nor the fecondary
ones about *Saturn*, *Jupiter*, and the Earth,
in concentrick Circles as they do, but
would have moved in Hyperbolas, or
Parabolas, or in Ellipfes very eccentrick.
To make this Syftem therefore, with
all its Motions, required a Caufe which
underftood, and compared together, the
Quantities of Matter in the feveral Bodies of the Sun and Planets, and the
gravitating Powers refulting from thence;
the feveral Diftances of the primary
Planets from the Sun, and of the fecondary ones from *Saturn*, *Jupiter*, and
the Earth; and the Velocities with which
thefe Planets could revolve about thofe
Quantities of Matter in the central Bodies, and to compare and adjuft all thefe
Things

Things together, in fo great a Variety of
Bodies, argues that Caufe to be not blind
and fortuitous, but very well fkilled in
Mechanicks and Geometry.

To your third Query, I anfwer, that
it may be reprefented that the Sun may,
by heating thofe Planets moft which are
neareft to him, caufe them to be better
concocted, and more condenfed by that
Concoction. But when I confider that
our Earth is much more heated in its
Bowels below the upper Cruft by fubter-
raneous Fermentations of mineral Bodies
than by the Sun, I fee not why the in-
terior Parts of *Jupiter* and *Saturn* might
not be as much heated, concocted, and
coagulated by thofe Fermentations as our
Earth is , and therefore this various Den-
fity fhould have fome other Caufe than
the various Diftances of the Planets from
the Sun. And I am confirmed in this
Opinion by confidering, that the Planets
of *Jupiter* and *Saturn*, as they are rarer
than

than the reft, fo they are vaftly greater,
and contain a far greater Quantity of
Matter, and have many Satellites about
them; which Qualifications furely arofe
not from their being placed at fo great
a Diftance from the Sun, but were rather
the Caufe why the Creator placed them
at great Diftance. For by their gravitating Powers they difturb one another's
Motions very fenfibly, as I find by fome
late Obfervations of Mr. *Flamfteed*, and
had they been placed much nearer to
the Sun and to one another, they would
by the fame Powers have caufed a confiderable Difturbance in the whole Syftem.

To your fourth Query, I anfwer, that
in the Hypothefis of Vortices, the Inclination of the Axis of the Earth might,
in my Opinion, be afcribed to the Situa-
tion of the Earth's Vortex before it was
abforbed by the neighbouring Vortices,
and the Earth turned from a Sun to a

C   Comet,

Comet; but this Inclination ought to decrease constantly in Compliance with the Motion of the Earth's Vortex, whose Axis is much less inclined to the Ecliptick, as appears by the Motion of the Moon carried about therein. If the Sun by his Rays could carry about the Planets, yet I do not see how he could thereby effect their diurnal Motions.

Lastly, I see nothing extraordinary in the Inclination of the Earth's Axis for proving a Deity, unless you will urge it as a Contrivance for Winter and Summer, and for making the Earth habitable towards the Poles; and that the diurnal Rotations of the Sun and Planets, as they could hardly arise from any Cause purely mechanical, so by being determined all the same way with the annual and menstrual Motions, they seem to make up that Harmony in the System, which, as I explaind above, was the Effect of Choice rather than Chance.

There

There is yet another Argument for a Deity, which I take to be a very ſtrong one, but till the Principles on which it is grounded are bettei received, I think it more adviſable to let it ſleep.

I am,

Your moſt humble Servant,

to command,

Cambridge,
Decemb. 10, 1692.

IS. NEWTON.

LETTER II.

For Mr. BENTLEY, *at the Palace at* Worcester.

SIR,

I Agree with you, that if Matter evenly diffused through a finite Space, not spherical, should fall into a solid Mass, this Mass would affect the Figure of the whole Space, provided it were not soft, like the old Chaos, but so hard and solid from the Beginning, that the Weight of its protuberant Parts could not make it yield to their Pressure. Yet by Earthquakes loosening the Parts of this Solid, the Protuberances might sometimes sink a little by their Weight, and thereby the Mass might, by Degrees, approach a spherical Figure.

The

The Reafon why Matter evenly fcat-
tered through a finite Space would convene in the midft, you conceive the fame
with me ; but that there fhould be a central Particle, fo accurately placed in the
middle, as to be always equally attracted
on all Sides, and thereby continue without Motion, feems to me a Suppofition
fully as hard as to make the fharpeft
Needle ftand upright on its Point upon a
Looking-Glafs. For if the very mathematical Center of the central Particle be
not accurately in the very mathematical
Center of the attractive Power of the
whole Mafs, the Particle will not be attracted equally on all Sides. And much
harder it is to fuppofe all the Particles in
an infinite Space fhould be fo accurately
poifed one among another, as to ftand
ftill in a perfect Equilibrium. For I reckon
this as hard as to make not one Needle
only, but an infinite number of them (fo
many as there are Particles in an infinite
Space) ftand accurately poifed upon their
Points.

Points. Yet I grant it poffible, at leaft by a divine Power; and if they were once to be placed, I agree with you that they would continue in that Pofture without Motion for ever, unlefs put into new Motion by the fame Power. When therefore I faid, that Matter evenly fpread through all Space, would convene by its Gravity into one or more great Maffes, I underftand it of Matter not refting in an accurate Poife.

But you argue, in the next Paragraph of your Letter, that every Particle of Matter in an infinite Space, has an infinite Quantity of Matter on all Sides, and by confequence an infinite Attraction every way, and therefore muft reft in Equilibrio, becaufe all Infinites are equal. Yet you fufpect a Paralogifm in this Argument; and I conceive the Paralogifm lies in the Pofition, that all Infinites are equal. The generality of Mankind confider Infinites no other ways than indefinitely;
and

and in this Senſe, they ſay all Infinites
are equal; tho' they would ſpeak more
truly if they ſhould ſay, they are neither
equal nor unequal, nor have any certain Difference or Proportion one to another. In this Senſe therefore, no Con-
cluſions can be drawn from them, about
the Equality, Proportions, or Differences
of Things, and they that attempt to do it
uſually fall into Paralogiſms. So when
Men argue againſt the infinite Diviſibility
of Magnitude, by ſaying, that if an Inch
may be divided into an infinite Number of
Parts, the Sum of thoſe Parts will be an
Inch, and if a Foot may be divided into
an infinite Number of Parts, the Sum of
thoſe Parts muſt be a Foot, and therefore
ſince all Infinites are equal, thoſe Sums
muſt be equal, that is, an Inch equal to
a Foot.

The Falſeneſs of the Concluſion ſhews
an Error in the Premiſes, and the Error
lies in the Poſition, that all Infinites are
equal.

equal. There is therefore another Way of considering Infinites used by Mathematicians, and that is, under certain definite Restrictions and Limitations, whereby Infinites are determined to have certain Differences or Proportions to one another. Thus Dr. *Wallis* considers them in his *Arithmetica Infinitorum*, where by the various Proportions of infinite Sums, he gathers the various Proportions of infinite Magnitudes : Which way of arguing is generally allowed by Mathematicians, and yet would not be good were all Infinites equal According to the same way of considering Infinites, a Mathematician would tell you, that tho' there be an infinite Number of infinite little Parts in an Inch, yet there is twelve times that Number of such Parts in a Foot, that is, the infinite Number of those Parts in a Foot is not equal to, but twelve Times bigger than the infinite Number of them in an Inch. And so a Mathematician will tell you, that if a

D   Body

Body ftood in Equilibrio between any two equal and contrary attracting infinite Forces, and if to either of thefe Forces you add any new finite attracting Force, that new Force, how little foever, will deftroy their Equilibrium, and put the Body into the fame Motion into which it would put it were thofe two contrary equal Forces but finite, or even none at all; fo that in this Cafe the two equal Infinites by the Addition of a Finite to either of them, become unequal in our ways of Reckoning, and after thefe ways we muft reckon, if from the Confiderations of Infinites we would always draw true Conclufions.

To the laft Part of your Letter, I anfwer, Firft, that if the Earth (without the Moon) were placed any where with its Center in the *Orbis Magnus*, and ftood ftill there without any Gravitation or Projection, and there at once were infufed into it, both a gravitating Energy towards the

the Sun, and a tranfverfe Impulfe of a juft Quantity moving it directly in a Tangent to the *Orbis Magnus*, the Compounds of this Attraction and Projection would, according to my Notion, caufe a circular Revolution of the Earth about the Sun. But the tranfverfe Impulfe muft be a juft Quantity; for if it be too big or too little, it will caufe the Earth to move in fome other Line. Secondly, I do not know, any Power in Nature which would caufe this tranfverfe Motion without the divine Aim. *Blondel* tells us fomewhere in his Book of Bombs, that *Plato* affirms, that the Motion of the Planets is fuch, as if they had all of them been created by God in fome Region very remote from our Syftem, and let fall from thence towards the Sun, and fo foon as they arrived at their feveral Orbs, then Motion of falling turned afide into a tranfverfe one. And this is true, fuppofing the gravitating Power of the Sun was double

at

at that Moment of Time in which they all arrive at their feveral Orbs; but then the divine Power is here required in a double refpect, namely, to turn the defcending Motions of the falling Planets into a fide Motion, and at the fame time to double the attractive Power of the Sun So then Gravity may put the Planets into Motion, but without the divine Power it could never put them into fuch a circulating Motion as they have about the Sun; and therefore, for this, as well as other Reafons, I am compelled to afcribe the Frame of this Syftem to an intelligent Agent.

You fometimes fpeak of Gravity as effential and inherent to Matter. Pray do not afcribe that Notion to me, for the Caufe of Gravity is what I do not pretend to know, and therefore would take more Time to confider of it.

I fear what I have faid of Infinites, will feem obfcure to you, but it is enough if
you

you underſtand, that Infinites when conſidered abſolutely without any Reſtriction or Limitation, are neither equal nor unequal, nor have any certain Proportion one to another, and therefore the Principle that all Infinites are equal, is a precarious one.

Sir, I am,

Your moſt humble Servant,

Trinity College,
Jan 17, 1692-3.

IS. NEWTON.

LETTER III.

For Mr. BENTLEY, *at the Palace at* Worcefter.

SIR,

BEcaufe you defire Speed, I will an-fwer your Letter with what Brevity I can. In the fix Pofitions you lay down in the Beginning of your Letter, I agree with you. Your affuming the *Orbis Mag-nus* 7000 Diameters of the Earth wide, implies the Sun's horizontal Parallax to be half a Minute. *Flamfteed* and *Caffini* have of late obferved it to be about 10", and thus the *OrbisMagnus* muft be 21,000, or in a rounderNumber 20,000 Diameters of the Earth wide. Either Computation I

think

think will do well, and I think it not worth while to alter your Numbers.

In the next Part of your Letter you lay down four other Positions, founded upon the six first. The first of these four seems very evident, supposing you take Attraction so generally as by it to understand any Force by which distant Bodies endeavour to come together without mechanical Impulse. The second seems not so clear; for it may be said, that there might be other Systems of Worlds before the present ones, and others before those, and so on to all past Eternity, and by consequence, that Gravity may be co-eternal to Matter, and have the same Effect from all Eternity as at present, unless you have somewhere proved that old Systems cannot gradually pass into new ones; or that this System had not its Original from the exhaling Matter of former decaying Systems, but from a Chaos of Matter evenly dispersed

difperfed throughout all Space ; for fomething of this Kind, I think, you fay was
the Subject of your fixth Sermon , and
the Growth of new Syftems out of old
ones, without the Mediation of a divine
Power, feems to me apparently abfurd.

The laft Claufe of the fecond Pofition
I like very well. It is inconceivable, that
inanimate brute Matter fhould, without
the Mediation of fomething elfe, which is
not material, operate upon, and affect
other Matter without mutual Contact, as
it muft be, if Gravitation in the Senfe of
Epicurus, be effential and inherent in it.
And this is one Reafon why I defired you
would not afcribe innate Gravity to me.
That Gravity fhould be innate, inherent
and effential to Matter, fo that one Body
may act upon another at a Diftance thro'
a *Vacuum*, without the Mediation of any
thing elfe, by and through which their
Action and Force may be conveyed from

E   one

one to another, is to me fo great an Ab-
furdity, that I believe no Man who has in
philofophical Matters a competent Faculty
of thinking, can evei fall into it. Gravity
muft be caufed by an Agent acting conftantly according to certain Laws ; but
whether this Agnt be material or immma-
terial, I have left to the Confideration of
my Readers.

Your fourth Affertion, that the World
could not be formed by innate Gravity
alone, you confirm by three Arguments.
But in your firft Argument you feem to
make a *Petitio Principii* ; for whereas
many ancient Philofophers and others, as
well Theifts as Atheifts, have all allowed,
that there may be Worlds and Parcels of
Matter innumerable or infinite, you deny
this, by reprefenting it as abfurd as that
there fhould be pofitively an infinite arith-
metical Sum or Number, which is a Contradiction *in Terminis* ; but you do not
prove

prove it as abfurd. Neither do you prove, that what Men mean by an infinite Sum or Number, is a Contradiction in Nature, for a Contradiction *in Terminis* implies no more than an Impropriety of Speech. Thofe things which Men underftand by improper and contradictious Phrafes, may be fometimes really in Nature without any Contradiction at all: a Silver Inkhorn, a Paper Lanthorn, an Iron Whetftone, are abfurd Phrafes, yet the Things fignified thereby, are really in Nature. If any Man fhould fay, that a Number and a Sum, to fpeak properly, is that which may be numbered and fummed, but Things infinite are numberlefs, or, as we ufually fpeak, innumerable and fumlefs, or infummable, and therefore ought not to be called a Number or Sum, he will fpeak properly enough, and your Argument againft him will, I fear, lofe its Force. And yet if any Man fhall take the Words, Number and Sum, in a larger Senfe, fo

as

as to underftand thereby Things, which
in the proper way of fpeaking are numberlefs and fumlefs (as you feem to do
when you allow an infinite Number of
Points in a Line) I could readily allow him
the Ufe of the contradictious Phrafes of
innumerable Number, or fumlefs Sum,
without inferring from thence any Abfur-
dity in the Thing he means by thofe
Phrafes. However, if by this, or any
other Argument, you have proved the
Finitenefs of the Univerfe, it follows, that
all Matter would fall down from the Out-
fides, and convene in the Middle. Yet
the Matter in falling might concrete into
many round Maffes, like the Bodies of
the Planets, and thefe by attracting one
another, might acquire an Obliquity of
Defcent, by means of which they might
fall, not upon the great central Body, but
upon the Side of it, and fetch a Compafs
about, and then afcend again by the fame
Steps and Degrees of Motion and Velocity

with

with which they defcended before, much after the Manner that the Comets revolve about the Sun, but a circular Motion in concentrick Orbs about the Sun, they could never acquire by Gravity alone.

And tho' all the Matter were divided at firft into feveral Syftems, and every Syftem by a divine Power conftituted like ours, yet would the Outfide Syftems defcend towards the Middlemoft; fo that this Frame of Things could not always fubfift without a divine Power to conferve it, which is the fecond Argument, and to your third I fully affent.

As for the Paffage of *Plato*, there is no common Place from whence all the Planets being let fall, and defcending with uniform and equal Gravities (as *Galileo* fuppofes) would at their Arrival to their feveral Orbs acquire their feveral Velocities, with which they now revolve in them.

them. If we fuppofe the Gravity of all
the Planets towards the Sun to be of fuch
a Quantity as it really is, and that the Motions of the Planets are turned upwards,
every Planet will afcend to twice its
Height from the Sun. *Saturn* will afcend till he be twice as high from the Sun
as he is at prefent, and no higher, *Jupiter* will afcend as high again as at prefent,
that is, a little above the Orb of *Saturn*;
Mercury will afcend to twice his prefent
Height, that is, to the Orb of *Venus*; and
fo of the reft, and then by falling down
again from the Places to which they afcended, they will arrive again at their feveral Orbs with the fame Velocities they
had at firft, and with which they now
revolve.

But if fo foon as their Motions by
which they revolve are turned upwards,
the gravitating Power of the Sun, by
which their Afcent is perpetually retarded,
be

be diminifhed by one half, they will now afcend perpetually, and all of them at all equal Diftances from the Sun will be equally fwift. *Mercury* when he arrives at the Orb of *Venus*, will be as fwift as *Venus*; and he and *Venus*, when they arrive at the Orb of the *Earth*, will be as fwift as the *Earth*, and fo of the reft. If they begin all of them to afcend at once, and afcend in the fame Line, they will conftantly in afcending become nearer and nearer together, and their Motions will conftantly approach to an Equality, and become at length flower than any Motion affignable. Suppofe therefore, that they afcended till they were almoft contiguous, and their Motions inconfiderably little, and that all their Motions were at the fame Moment of Time turned back again; or, which comes almoft to the fame Thing, that they were only deprived of their Motions, and let fall at that Time, they would all at once arrive at their feveral Orbs, each

with

with the Velocity it had at firft; and if their Motions were then turned Sideways, and at the fame Time the gravitating Power of the Sun doubled, that it might be ftrong enough to retain them in their Orbs, they would revolve in them as before their Afcent. But if the gravitateing Power of the Sun was not doubled, they would go away fiom their Orbs into the higheft Heavens in parabolical Lines. Thefe Things follow from my *Princ. Math. Lib.* 1. *Prop.* 33, 34, 36, 37.

I thank you very kindly for your defigned Prefent, and reft

Your moft

humble Servant

to command,

Cambridge,
Feb. 25, 1692-3.

IS. NEWTON.

LETTER IV.

To Mr. BENTLEY, *at the Palace at* Worcester.

SIR,

THE Hypothesis of deriving the Frame of the World by mechanical Principles from Matter evenly spread through the Heavens, being inconsistent with my System, I had considered it very little before your Letters put me upon it, and therefore trouble you with a Line or two more about it, if this comes not too late for your Use.

In my former I represented that the diurnal Rotations of the Planets could not be derived from Gravity, but required a divine Arm to impress them. And tho'

F   Gravity

Gravity might give the Planets a Motion of Defcent towards the Sun, either directly or with fome little- Obliquity, yet the tranfverfe Motions by which they revolve in their feveral Orbs, required the divine Arm to imprefs them according to the Tangents of their Orbs. I would now add, that the Hypothefis of Matter's being at firft evenly fpread through the Heavens, is, in my Opinion, inconfiftent with the Hypothefis of innate Gravity, without a fupernatural Power to reconcile them, and therefore it infers a Deity. For if there be innate Gravity, it is impoffible now for the Matter of the Earth and all the Planets and Stars to fly up from them, and become evenly fpread throughout all the Heavens, without a fupernatural Power, and certainly that which can never be hereafter without a fupernatural Power, could never be heretofore without the fame Power.

You

You queried, whether Matter evenly
fpread throughout a finite Space, of fome
other Figure than fpherical, would not in
falling down towards a central Body,
caufe that Body to be of the fame Figure
with the whole Space, and I anfwered,
yes. But in my Anfwer it is to be fup-
pofed that the Matter defcends directly
downwards to that Body, and that that
Body has no diurnal Rotation.

This, Sir, is all I would add to my
former Letters.

I am,

Your moft humble

Servant,

Cambridge,
Feb. 11, 1693.

IS. NEWTON.

F I N I S.

www.ingramcontent.com/pod-product-compliance
Lightning Source LLC
Chambersburg PA
CBHW061239260626
47172CB00003B/928